T0365334

# POEMS
## from
# CAPTAIN SALTY'S

## Crumbles of Piecemeal Pie

### Michael P. Amram

**North America & international**
toll-free: 1 888 232 4444 (USA & Canada)
fax: 812 355 4082

# Introduction

Bawdiness tempts the poet who trusts complacency. Risqué is the poet who mixes innuendos with lyrical poetry. *Poems from Captain Salty's: crumbles of piecemeal pie* lacks the flow of eroticism the eye is trained to see—or at least expect—in poetry books. The good captain had other interests. These come out of the blasé poems included in this book and I implore the reader to compare them to the more suggestive, satiating digestive fare served elsewhere in Captain Salty's. I ask the reader to contrast the mundane chaste poems with those that nudge nuances of censorship. Those handfuls of innocent poems are the gentle sorbets I hope will make readers aware of the more suggestive crèmes. The naughty ones arrive at the table's edge, like pills too curious to simply swallow with swill. The bawdy ones are a tease. The naughtier ones, it's come to my attention, are pleasing to the eyes of some readers.

I thumbed through a book of erotic poetry. For several weeks *The Poetic Art of Seduction* (Pleasure Portal Press, 2103) remained at the top in the poetry books of a chart I saw. I remember being surprised someone would—or could—deliver an entire book of salacious verse. The sampling I read was very suggestive and sensual. *Seduction* overtly displays eroticism with continuity and no apparent "safe" word while *Captain Salty's* appetite is sated by the odd entendre or innuendo. What's never, or almost never, said is what compels people to read what they read. I have never read *Fifty Shades of Gray* and I doubt I will. I do, however, find it interesting that there was such feverous reading of the book. Was it our puritanical origin that is left in the virginal few? Perhaps it was the language used to detail the absence of computer images of people engaged in acts of an erotic nature. I would not write a book of a consistently erotic nature. I doubt I could.

It was suggested to me once that women are less visually inclined. Reading and imagining sex and/or eroticism is stimulation enough. Men, conversely, need or want pictures, and purchase a magazine or turn on a computer screen. It was a generalization, born out of the persistent question of which sex is more cerebral. I will not offer any definite answer, although women do often come out on top.

My last novel, *Agent of Orange*, tells a multi-faceted story of complex characters, each seeking closure in life. There are elements of eroticism, but they are story- bound. The naughty bits are consequences of the characters, who they are, and what they do.

*Poems from Captain Salty's* is a smattering of sex and innuendoes interjected liberally between the main courses of poetry. Its offerings can be as chaste as a poem concerning papal ascension and white smoke rising from the Vatican chimney:

"cassocks wrinkle, diphthongs sound
guttural until popes realize
black smoke rising bold
from Vatican chimneys to
holy skies Rome tries to hide

silver hammers tap heads
that can nod, they writhe
and feel for traces of papal left,
then call for silence as chalk
scratches boards to nominate them…"

(from "good saint Hugo")

Captain Salty probes society's tolerance levels. He questions permissiveness while watching whose teeth need picking at the end of the meal. He oscillates the poems and waits for heads to turn from the tamer ones and sneak furtive glances at erotic and anatomic puns. *Poems from*
*Captain Salty's* is sliced as liberally as a poem about a war correspondent choosing isolation over betraying his country:

"they told him to stay in there
in his hideaway,
to decorate his pied-à-terre
with things he'd never see

with guns and blunt implements
he was to stay there
to lie and wait out a war
with the late Billy Shears. . ."

(from "piecemeal pie")

I invite you to peruse the seas with Captain Salty, aided by the keen insight of his glass eye and heightened sense for balance in the world from walking on pegged legs. I hope your finds spark discussion, wonderment, and illusion.

Bon voyage.

# Table of Contents

To those who nurtured me along the way,

To all who stood to make the trip worth my effort—

# Phonetics

"I love you"
is the
salutation,
three words
often
abridged to
one;

"love…" ends
missives
to relations
in place
of phrases
that sound
trite and done

I fear two words
might not be
returned,
like footnotes
lead to
catch-phrases
I read

I search
expressions
of agape
love in
letters sent
that end well
with arms
hugging

"I love you"
stood by
for fill-in blanks
when "love"
was not enough,
or "love you"
dangled thoughts
to tell

so I didn't
speak what
I meant to
say, my breath
is held
to be expelled
someday

# Valentine's Day Massacre

His nose was nary to breach the bar,
It was set high to measure a sneeze and
Time its velocity, to gauge its propensity
To manipulate loose–lipped patrons
Arriving past happy-hours;

They fingered i-phones suspiciously
To report happenings in bars
Like sneezes beyond sound barrier's
Speed that warp letters that
Patrons' eyes can spell;

The do-gooders, the Samaritans,
Robbers of pleasantries who
Surmise worst case scenarios
Of a dining experience that's
Ruined before the bill arrives;

So he nipped at his beer slowly,
All cool, like he waited for
A limousine to take him far, where
Faces had mugs that wouldn't stare
At reflections in rails of bars;

The patrons rose to assist
Him like the amiable lush
Who came to sit for a spell of
I.O.U. to pigs on radios that
Had to report what they saw fly
Over their heads on Valentine 's Day.

# Stool Pigeons

I sat rigid
for the briefing,
the rules were
explained
because I'd
left dashes
for tips
when I dined

I left
unintentionally,
I swore at
a couple
of times,
I owed them
tips--shit,
and then at
night in bed
it dawned
to me that
I paid

A list existed
because of
oscillations
I made, the
ways I moved
from stool
to stool,

unconsciously
hoping my
tab was paid
through osmosis
and the dims
of dexterity

I flew under
radars of
brown eyes
that knew me,
they grew wise
and shook
so I'd
"settle up"
and move to
a different place

I'll admit
I had a
modus
operandi,
It was a
subliminal
contempt
with the intent
of confusing
them

my brain traded
metaphors
for money, drink
and realities
who were the
phonies I met

I'd fidget
and they thought
of nice things
to say to me,
fu--ing
saccharine words
cobbled for
the rube who
might appreciate
them someday,
they'd drink
to talk and
when I rose
to shuffle away
the barkeep
lent me his
sobriety
to thwart games
I was known
to play.

# Nature's Vagabonds

They wander, communing with
Nature in southern France—
Seven strong women preen;

Glancing naked at the cools
Of shadows under the
Overpass— lost the nymphs dance

And breasts draw awkward
Attention to their coy
Curly hairs studying the ground

They toe the cobblestones in
Flip-flops and slippers they
Jam with penetrable force

White or pink hair bands hold
Their small heads up, and the alpha
Nymph who whiles the septet on the

Hour's ways, proceeding unashamed,
Daring voyeurs' eyefuls,
They amend themselves to hide

An oeuf– like sunny side nipple
Vagabonds trolling Nice's bridges to
Catch a glimpse of sun for them.

# Symbiosis

you said there was
a reason you
were here,
on earth to be
held for so long
you'd tear

it's undisputed,
the title worn
so proud
like a champion belt
boxers hold
so high

still you maintain
a trusted poise,
silent,
with dignity
like ships moor
to stay
on course with the
tides that fray sharp
edges

so I hold you
near as you laugh
to grin,
it's still undisputed—
the cheer I helped
you win

I hold you close
so the earth
will spin,
for seasons to
turn leaves to see
you grin

# Television gods

You promised church services would not be televised
And said there'd be no ulterior motive,
God would be live—

But antenna ears received you, they knew you'd bow
Your head, and nod in time with a tube so
Thoughts fused with plasma TV—

I pretended our breakfast nook was a pew and I watched;
I nodded to caution you and whatever ghosts sat
In the room with us—

I said "be quiet or he won't come out you know,"
I instructed a parish couple who were
Settled in for the show—

I mentioned how Glenda (the good witch) waved
A wand to entice munchkins out to confess
Their love of lollipop guilds—

God was there, somewhere reciprocating your trance,
Scrutinizing how air waves dance behind the toupée of
An evangelist—

A conduit deceived you with hair that flapped at
Moments timed to the thorny crown he wore
As a messenger,

You offered donations for his presence in houses
With nooks and allowing god
To scintillate the air.

# Their Longevity

she tendered me
with balls,
crystal sifted dull
smoky hazes
that churned small
bits of me
into glow

I sat like
Frankenstein
with neck
bolts tight
to stifle
my eye's
instincts to roll

I had doubts
and pondered
legitimacy
of sons
or daughters,
I wondered if
her crumbled
coffers bore
progeny

purple pastels
and stars in
scarves held
her face
tight, I saw
her wink
and smile

she waved to
me with
wrists that
jangled above
from tarnished
bracelets

dim lights shed
what consumed
a tent,
they were the
brass rings I
reached when
my money
was spent

my mistrust
of her led
me far, to
places I once
knew, confined
spaces where talk
was cheap
and eyes of
truer blue glowed
and sagged cheeks
of gypsies
who are
hanged for
telling
fortunes right

I let Madame's
tent flaps hang,
I exposed
her private
parts so she
winked demure
in dims of light
that shined up
through sags
bought by
the less
fortunate sons

# Revisions

I'll track down a date to reinvent my time,
I'll know passages that teach futures to wait,
Time passes through walls channeling ghosts in
The TV sets that buzzed in the waiting room;

So I'll change my ways to re– discover the
Lessons that reflected my yesterdays;

Time's bastard's born free, with tomorrows to learn
And decades to burn a child bouncing
On oblivion's knee and life still peeked each way as it
Crossed the street to ignore,

I'll search for the days in history when knees buckled but life
Still fit the corners it frayed, where crinoline slipped from sheets
I wore so time knocked me aware of my confidence.

# Feeding Underdogs

swallowing our
pride took
time, it
involved rhythm
to ingest
pedestrian
pills that
followed the
less recommended
vitamins

they were
chewable
like the ones
Underdog
kept in his ring
to rescue
his sweet Polly
from Simon
and Cad

they were a
shine boy's
medications
for identity,
orange pills
for extraordinary
times life
navigates
far too close

pills that saved
matches of

socks that
multiplied
or match-box
cars that
defiled us
like cheese
slicer's wires

they were those
hand-held
devices that
produced
Velveeta
with ease
in thick
creamy
slices

they slid off
long blocks
magically
without guides
of gauging
metaphors
to limit
accuracy
and make us
wonder if our
bread was pure

in the 70s
the crusts got
cut off and
bread was
so white they
found solace
in the plate,

and kids
could relate
to things like
lost heroes
on TV

the bread bounced
off images
that swam
on the plates,
Like Casey
Jones shuffling
across in
his winter
underwear

lunch time fasted
our minds
'til we rooted
for a cat
to foil
Riff Raff's plans,
and we'd take
a pill
again to
be sure that
savior-fare
was everywhere

# SCUBA

Amidst coral's sediment silt where sea kelp waves and emerald suns are felt
Life purges weightlessly breathing blind to deaf but mute to see
Lost souls reaching for fluidity

They follow their bubbles' flow and watch for their bursts to see airs
Of their ways, they look for garden's serenity, where legends are
Hanged for complicity

It's where the second guessers go, the depths that the enslaved
Yes-men and people pleasers know, where they go and
Think to stew like crusted prawns

It's where broths bubble to blend space with time and life rejects those
In line for second takes, for souls that lost searching
For the Fred Flintstone breaks

And then time changes direction and oceans feel apparatuses
Underwater breathing allows for second
Chances

# Parental Guidance

From the shores
of Gichigami
tides came in
loudly lapping,
they went out
again
with precise
cadence
like tumblers
give locks
to rise,

or tight lines
acrobats pad
thin to
compromise
integrity,
the great lake flushed
for father's day to
the tide's
ebbing;

its foam crackled
above
the wind, its fish
smell found
our cabin,

it knew the
place, a little
domicile on
Tofte's knolls
keeping
me safe

I slid a tape
recorder
under his
bed one night
to capture
sounds of
snoring
denied the
previous night

he said it
sounded "like
the sea" as I
played it back
in the morning
on father's day

# Features of Habit

They implore you to touch finesse
As drips slip right, you grip firm,
Glass's heat tempers you
To the physics of coffee urns;

And mornings crack wise to your wrist
So carpe diem knows your yawns
And then water warms
Up through physics of coffee urns;

It's a sieved carafe that never laughs
At tricks you refused to learn,
And wins squeezed into
Fresh each morning as your fingers
Mold their urn,

You tilt it right, you raise it tight
To splash like divers try
In a réservoir
For the physics of coffee urns

Then filters do the rest for you,
You slip in bed and wait
As you cup gets filled
By the physics of coffee urns.

# Lizzy

she wore a crown,
a tiara
had different
purposes,
to her it
had sapphire studs
but she ignored
what wealth
followed her

she worried so much
about her image
as she fled
the heist with
a cape of red hair
trailing her
to leave something
to camouflage

she panicked
to bum some heat
from them,
her captors watched
as she lit a
cigarette
in a yahrtzeit
candle's
flame to show
indifference

she punctuated
her nonchalance
with death or
incarcerated
sentences she'd do

captors combed
her red mane
for colors
that ran as
she smoked

and the casual
affair she
had with death
lagged and feigned
concern
while she dragged
each breath in
her head

the captors watched
and gauged time
by the rise
and falls
of her chest,
they heard fleas
drop from hair
left unwashed
purposely

a car she drove
to chase spots
of desert sun
was throttled
wildly as
though the horizon
knew how
death should be.

# Pecking Orders

who's the alpha dog?
one who defends
bows to him,
who's the alpha dog?

the cat who
keeps his cool
locked up,
he's a puss
in tights who
envies the
highs in life,

he's that aphasic
man who
hums low in
a box to pleasure
his wife;

who are alpha dogs?
they're in line to wager
their worth,
he scrutinizes an i-pad
as eyes squint

he thinks when
sex happened
first and his
women used beta
to tell who
the top dogs are
with barks
greater than
bites they fear,
the cats
who stand up
so cool to nip at
bottles of beer,

the alpha dog rubs
off last night's
commendations
that he saved,
his woman
spoons him
with beta
prowess and knows
he's afraid.

# Suffragettes

someone
wanted Joan,
the pride
of women was
at stake

she felt
porous
wisps for
divinity,
beams of light
men wink to
see

at first her
blood boiled
and she guessed
whose call
she'd answer

so she
calculated
when effects
of her nudges
of equality
might take

she multi-tasked
to evade
the questions
God might ask
and His blows
of smoke
fueled her
way

smoke clouds
parted, sun
pierced
her eyes,
flames waxed
at her
brows, they
beat her
until she
was certain
He'd see

# Rebellious lines

I rubbed in
temples
for luck of him
and me,
they felt swell
with oily
pimpled
faces,

we massaged
traces of
skin that
erupted
to spread
like lessons
scooped from
incandescent
jars of cream

I calculated
their worth,
their resistance
to appeal
and deduce
pimples
I'd pop
if my
face could
malign his

the mirror's
man waved
to me,
articulating
my words so
the cream began
to burn and
infect things
I could
not see;

I connected
the dots like
an insecure
leopard might,
and my voice
cracked so he'd
hear me right.

# Shelf-lives

I'll wring out the last months
Like a sponge to make it to fifty
In the comforting shadow of a hill,
With its inclinations that flavor suns
Peppering them with hallucinations
So my mind will ask if life's
Half over or half begun.

I'll wring months out, I'll bring
Them out and twist their ends like bags
Of bread for freshness

I'll look back and sigh to
Regret time spent in hasted ways,
I'll consider the falls and the
Lessons I ignored just because
I thought I was brave

And I'll judge whether any
Of the first half was wasted
Not seasoned to tastes of time
I willed to the shadow that grew
On a hill's slope to save;
I'll wring them out well, god,
I'll sing them with the might's I've
Reserved for mid-life crises
Like these.

# Hoodwinking Death

She fought to deceive her hooded fallacies
Like death's fickle pecker,
She never thought she'd live to know
Men who swam free inside her;

She felt like a kindred phantom pleasured her each
Time a moyl licked his
Scalpel clean to eviscerate skin that grew
So death lingered longer
Without hoods revealing the private parts they knew;

SHE SQUEAKS, SHE SIGHS, AND SHE WINCES
In her pain, a prima
Donna pro tem who codifies her will to last
Amend—she remembers life;

She's collecting her useless skins like
Appendices and
Only by death's amendments can she let men
Be repealed by knives;

When the hoods are off, she points out blame,
Her fingers creak the swollen prominences
She tries to explain;

All the missionaries who lost sleep for her,
Then prayed for her, and
Waded through bloody sheets she pounded on rocks
As she danced to slake the rain;

SHE SQUEAKS, SHE MOANS, SHE DROWNS
She remembers lives
In casualties afforded for her
Hymen's sake, for clues of
Her unflinching trust in death's sterility.

# Distant Relationships

Things were never real, like when hurricanes dance in
Eyes to change worlds so nature offers options
But still some orthodox boys stand as Tallitot lash
Their arms to their sides to suppress nature's beast

But I could see Sahara's sands drifting by me, and I chose one
Granule to be my wife, and it was revealed in Sanskrit
Babbles of a shaman I knew, "*vasati saparyati
Tvattanat zraddha, strota deva madhye*"
His dying words were that I live a separate life

He said I should find hurricane eyes to warn me not
Allow god to linger inside too long, he cautioned me
Never to close my eyes at night if some arms resist
Lashes secured to coax my wife to take trips separately,

They are never real, the holy unions that blind weary souls
Mute in ways they pray, a document is signed, it's kissed by
God, it's the covenant fear comes from; and hash marks start
To burn and lead pathways to savor together's days.

# Role Playing

She left me a few to use, a roll or two to keep
Safe and high in a place dry and out of reach;
She rolled hers under each time to confuse gravity, and then tore
Squares off quickly to feel the fan they made

But my roll was always on lease, it was my responsibility;
My TP was rationed, it was savored
Until she asked me where it went, how she always got ahead of
Me in passive mind-game we played

She sat on her throne whipping squares under, scoffing laws of
Physics she hoped tight sphincters obeyed,
So I crouched at her throne crossing my legs as she prayed to
Utter words gods tickled her uvula to say:

Like how paper rolls should fall to last throughout her weeks;
Or how squares torn quickly know their fans;
She analyzed me her best and I guessed what crazy shit her
Quivering lips had slipped to reimburse retentiveness—

But then I considered the rationality she lost to close the deal
And seal the lid so I stayed home more often

# Principle Friends

high school learned
trivial things,
incredulous in
a yearbook's
random signings

jocks pounded geeks,
brains figured how
to get somewhere
if they cliqued right

freaks hid
their weed
in bathroom
waste bins,
alarms
sounded
to say grow
higher then

jocks stood
holding
big red
dodge balls
to smack geeky
faces hard
and wimpy

and eyes
knew picture
days always
blurred to
to gimpy
but a
negative
was saved

in thirty
years you
revisit them,
the kids
in the
hall that
tormented you

at hotel
pool sides
drunk women
scratch at
the other's
clothes to
dance on laps;

cheerleaders
and homecoming
queens, the
girls who
never
gave you
a first glance

the girls
you knew
who opened
their minds
to no one
but you
back then

reunions now
fit you
in cool
and slim
as jocks
lament hairs
of principal
friends

# Letterman Jackets

you traded
hands with
finesse
and rounded
circles in
a singlet

your seat hung
tight from
suspenders
your opponents
snapped to
agitate you;

they crouched down
and sneered
from well-drilled
stances like
spring– loaded
traps set
for you

they shuffled
around in
soft- shoed patter
on spongy mats
that smacked
you hard like
sweat socks
filled with
pennies

in high school
you lettered
JV,
you wrestled
state meets
to satisfy then
and pinned
a letter
on a board you had—
but never bought
a jacket
for it to wear

glory days
blink possible
pasts and you
grapple with
hands' faking
trades to care
and patterns
on sofas
fill your head
with images
of cauliflower ears
symbols of
failed dances
with speed,
gnarled ghosts
you fought once
to someday need

# #Hashtag 1984

time was on your
side then,
big brother looked
down on you
misguiding you,
making sure you
abided by the rules of diversity,

he sided with the
"freedom is slavery"
mentality
we'd seen in our roots,
so where were you
in 1984?

prince was pontificating
perversity
and we'd get
crazy to get to
the after-life,
purified by
Minneapolis lakes
divinity

people fanned larger
hairs girls could spray,
they just wanted
to have fun
with giant men
with rubber bands
in beards stroked
to indicate how
a girl's work was done,

so there we were,
the legendary class
of '84
we'd wait like pylons
in parallel parking
lanes in Eagan where
the test was easier

orange became
red in our caps
and gowns flowing
to Met Center pomp
as we crossed
the stage to receive
our sheepskin pat.

then RHS doors
locked behind us,
we partied all night
without a drink,
and Van Halen
told us to jump
so we obliged,
and morning's halls
were strewn with
tassels and bands
hair couldn't save.

# Shear Will of Man

I talked myself into letting
her mess with my head
she guaranteed
"you'll be a feral man,"
that's all Delila said

I'd read of Sampson's strength
of one, or more, hairs cut
by vengeful women who wielded sheers
over a soul's command;

Delilah cut seven as he slept
peaceful in her lap,
in the fruit of her loins where last
rites of men are trapped

I measured its length and
my worth as a hairy man,
I guessed it was less in bulk
than the strength of single strands.

# Piecemeal Pie

they told him to stay in there
in his hideaway,
to decorate his pied-à-terre
with things he'd never see

with guns and blunt implements
he was to stay there
to lie and wait out a war
with the late Billy Shears

he had a good run at fame
and fortunes that come
when you envy a name
that plays on your fears

they told him to stew inside,
to think about things
and occupy countries with
his ideologies.

# Easy Riders

combing through
America,
"long-hairs" tweezed
as they rode past
revving their
mutton chops,

Captain Americas
contested captains
of America
in races to
individual freedom

hair pitted the
truly free
against those
too shorn to see
what's not there

captains born
to learn how
free they
aren't, they
comb America

they're last seen
searching for
freedoms,
frees of money
frees of color

they scan skies to
reign frees,
for iced drips
of freedom
to complain

for sovereignty
of free ideas
and to envy
the long hairs'
freedom

Captain America
goes
south to die
a little,
past lost
souls of saints

and Fonda hugged
Mary complacently
as though an
American dream
waits in wombs

ideals are
conceived
immaculately
down south
to remain
out of reach

it's a
virgin,
the dream's
a mascaraed
whore,
and captains
rape her
freedoms

they're the
highest
men of
America
who search for
bumps to rise

abutments
in roads
or grooms
to comb
bellies when
dreams
compromise

this land is theirs,
it's everything
they'll never see,
it's everything
they can't be

'cause they're
captains
of America,
they are the
shills of industry

and America
dies a little
to be free,
to search that
road so well
like Kerouac

long hairs part
the middle
of America
its captain
saved to sell.

# This Land is my Land

so I strolled
along
the highway
rubbing the
chrome of
cars until
it glowed

I searched
for faces
of reflected
stares I drew.

I bartered
for the two
chrome plates
I was owed.

they asked me
how to handle
my holey
gloves I wore

if I should
be approached
at the
exit ramp
at all to
even the score

I confessed,
I cheated
on the test
panhandlers take

the quiz drifters
fake to beat
their odds
of living right

a life with
means well
beyond what
it gives

so I repeated
my answers
with subtle clues
that shined

reflections in
cars I used
to see if I'd
wasted time.

# Anger's Man

He dances
from the weight
of elephants
and sings
contemporary
songs
biting at
satire
with yellow
teeth

ignorance
is bliss, his
boney face
sneering
relentless Fs
as he preaches

angry man, angry man
spare a hand if you can

ignorance
is bliss when
a Buddhist begs
revolution,
when he plots
to overthrow
his government

he leads down paths
that rant to cite
irrelevant history
he pulls from
a featherless fedora
worn too much
to protest

angry man, angry man
squinting to watch
what he can

ignorance
is bliss when
a man lives
too suspiciously
and sleeps
soundly with
his guns

he's a survivalist,
who'd rewrite
history,
he was
born too
late and
missed his
opportunities
to embrace
upheaval

to make
things right,
before text
messages helped
throw fights
before NSA
could listen
and win

angry man, angry man
walks with his staff
and handles pans

his diet
consists of
macro
biology
and he
skulks gaunt,
his feet drag
animating him
like a
puppeteer

ignorance
is bliss when
angry man never
gets ahead to win
he just humors
us with toothy grins.

# Franks

in white-washed
shacks
edging towns,
a lone bulb
swings, it
bats at flies
that go around

they slip through
cracks society
opens,
graciously
salting wounds

sanity hides
for seeks
to smell where
the wind blows
so stench eats
at them
until they
see

the fecal
matter smears
walls with
letters that
swirl threats
cursively,

for some franks
are just
parasites
with stories
over doors
to tell

*"f--k you!"*
culminates cracks,
it dries
hard trusted
anger
and leaves
wanting more. . .

*"shit on it*
*if you got some"*
paints murals
on doors,
prayers that
wishing
will work

like when
Sundays were
spent to
remember
what Jesus said
before he died;

when it
was decided
whether he
lied, and
folks were
really
on their own
and no one
cared to
address
wounds inflicted
by society,

to confess
gaps in
mental health
that keep
homeless sane
in excremental
white-washed shacks. . .

# Zoroastrian Tenderness

it was in your time
of dying
when we first met;
and you smiled
through brightly
colored
crocodile tears

they fell to wet
pages that nimbly
mimed your turns,
it was alright
with me if you
let others read

your secret's safe,
ways you'd defend
me to refine
your dignity,
I expect nothing
else from you

you sighed and made
jokes to laugh
at things
that I mused,
so you praised
me glibly,
it felt alright

you offered me
conciliatory hugs
and dyed scarves
from your wardrobe
and eternal
spirit of good

you took selfies
to pose cute
it's alright love,
your brash
expressions and
funny faces
read stories
so well.

# Pandora's Vineyard

I poured out
my soul
so you'd stomp
on it like grapes
until your feet
felt blue

and you shared
some wine,
drams of drips
lying there
like leaves
vines reach on days
when we are
simpatico
enough to
hear each other,
when we're bold
enough for fear

to forsake
the other,
when you'd
consent to
teach me to
cry your ways

but I offered
my heart,
tight like a coffin
sealed for eternity,
I opened it
and you laughed

I pried at it
you held me
and lied,
Pandora
I'm sorry I
opened for you

I was bold,
your feet were blue
but cold and
nimble to skip
compatibility;
you prefer
life closed,
earth–bound as
coffins should be.

# Masking Tapes

He sat alone to pick his head
'Til it leaked the matter he trusted,
He pried loose what had dried like
Discarded cut crusts of wonder bread;

He goggled an i-device so well
It burned crosses in his mind,
Little kicks brains seldom tell
Like coagulants for time;

He threw his hands, he talked tough,
And ladled stories thick like
A bravado soup stirs with
Popped pustules that ooze
From brain–celled stems of
Broccoli florets,
He blew soft on a spoon to
Cool his racist tendencies
That judged bowls for depth;

So he sat to let her blow some,
To cradle his leaking matter
And laugh with him and pick
His brain to hear of fights he'd won.

# Finishing school

next to a
Finnish sauna
was a hole
in the ice,
jagged edges
knew our way
in and out
quickly,
to splash
numb
moments
that burned
like our
shivers
guided stars

huddles
of women
came fast
around
the sauna
naked
and politely
asked we
look the
other way,
they looked
ashamed
of things
men might
see or think
to say

we stripped
ourselves
in the
absence of
modesty
but the
women
loitered
and peeked
awkwardly

we lodged
in sweat,
smoke rose
like our
carcasses
smoldered
murderous
intents

we felt lost
after
our first plunge
had won,
when our
retreats
from lake
holes had
begun,

then I saw
a dozen
soles jump
feet first
into the night,
white balls
streaked
snow and
moons were high
and hands
waved free,
it was
a sextet of men
probably

they took off
across
the lake and
left globes
of snow swirls
for their
wake, I
did not
count heads
or eyes
that they
could see

# Winning by a Nose

you took one
on the chin
for sycophants,
you wore black
face to brown
their nose to
kiss a better class
someday

you spoofed
their minstrel shows
so someone dared
to wear
white suits
and top hats
that covered eyes
and tails that
dusted your past

you kept your
nose clean
to be aware
of Uncle Tom,
and you stared
at pale faces
when eyes rolled
laughter into
small sockets

then skin cleared,
it peeled
like bibles end
in revelations
that permit
tears to shoes'
tapping toes
when darkness shines
in shadows

images of
peoples' applause
for imitations,
the star-struck
eyes of their
pensive grins,
still you followed
your nose to
spite memories
of minstrel shows.

# A Sense of Righteousness

a vacuum
licked its prey
and you felt safe
because the
mites were dead
so your
bloodhound
scratched its
naughty bits
and played

his tail wagged
once to
signal
his master,
and a rocking
chair moved
closer to
its tail,
curtains slimmed
in silence,
and began
to sway
and carpet
sweepers
threatened dogs
tails left
alone to play

the hound dog
rose to
shake its
pink jowls and
upstaged
monotony of
the day;

and the rocking
chair wove
complicity
as a sampler
was stitched

a servant
picked trusted
threads that
hid things
you hoped your
guests could
see

your hound found
places that
bitches
hid their
confidence
you trusted
so natural
and timely
from days you spent
sweeping mites

you had some
small sense
the house-boy
should lift the
dog's tail
to peek for
shadows he
threw so well
from the hands
that stitched
samples
of stories
pink jowls tell.

# The Circus Mime

He commands the stage in pantaloons
And teardrops painted on his face,
A hobo hat is turned up to affect,
To elicit sympathy from clowns
Who never made it big, never jumped
And left the impact that shoes of
Clowns can have

He wavers back and forth, his voice slides
With silence, scintillating like pond ripples
To show he's brave and his voice reverberates
Arena walls, his eyes close to let fans' lighters
Flicker like matchsticks rubbed furtively, he
Wades waist deep in crowds that claw him
With arms that are blind to him, so he squints
In lights to catch their trips;

Back and forth he arches to them, in and out
He isolates, he desecrates the stage louder still
But whisper peaks pay bills, and fans know
He wears that desperation from curbed
Temptations, from flagellations of salad days

His curtains call for bows, for him to grin
With diamonds in his teeth

He twists back and forth in dervish
Whirls, pig-tail curls, like sovereign flags
Unfurl when fans begin to wave

He's isolated, he's desiccated with sacks
In his pockets of stage fright, it's anticipated
So he rocks. . .

Back and forth, on or off the scale
That sinks stars that never waited,
Rocking slower, his clown feats trip him,
Mascara is dripping and lights that spot
Pantaloons slip like moths from flames.

# Entrepreneurs

monkeys
feel rhythms
of their trials,
nudges
from masters
who know where
they've been,
monkeys sense
vibrations of
slow trains
and dance
on instinct
to inherit
their wind,

aping coolness
of the underground,
random
rhythms are heard
in tunnels,
sounds trains make
like harmonies
monkeys fake
to the end

you rubbed until
your monkey
saw his reflection
in dimes he
busked
for you, like
an estranged
relation who
must sit in
a corner and
think about what
he did.

# Aurora Borealis

emptiness lasted
his highways
so the truck
pushed to overdrive,
he prayed hard
to calculate
when he'd arrive

fleeting across
Saskatchewan
highway lines
blurred to speak
Canadian French

his truck shined
shimmering off
Alberta's dew
so he told
his mirror
a French phrase
he knew

he'd come far
from Chicago
following
his dreams
with a prayer
not to have
to use his
extended
thumb

he lamented
lost legs,
trips never
learned well,
like the tale
of Buffalo
he loved to tell
and how the
border guards
had encouraged
him to
explore
the ways
c'est la vie
translates well

# Isolating aspirations

In retirement I'll shake off my mantle,
The mélange of successes I've had
That gave me a sense of taste,
My books will be expired like overdue
periodicals people slide into a depository,
So I promise to write faster
With salience and clarity to recoup my dues

I'm Salinger writing without the seaweed
Life grows like to snarl and taunt with to
Expedite their yield, so I
Wait for it to float past book plots that I weaved,
I'm Thoreau pondering cracks, sneering down knot-holes
At writes to block so I have a clear shot at
Hanging my toes in Caribbean

I warm to the grandest Cayman that listens
To me, that provides simple pleasures and
Inspires me to tap out
Essays based on barmaids at a Hard Rock
Café with guitars on the walls that reverberate
To angle the faces I see

I walk Church Street's cobble, stoned perusing
George Town's latest happy feet, kicking through
Crumbles of tax-free concrete,
I sift for stories to tell, to show one barmaid
And offer some tip to her when I
Leave the café.

# Ballad of Captain Solomon Salty

One man sailed all seven seas
in search of one slice of pie
to find a piece to call on
down "a vast ye mates I spy!"

On a bow sprite with hair,
sallow, ripe with scurvy,
Safe in her crow's nest
Sol lived out his fantasy

oh, the good captain!
alas, spirits ate his pride
oh, that fine captain!
through glass squints are eyed

One man fought seas in vein
to find a kinder love,
Beyond siren's captivations
to spy crow's feet above

Solomon's a lissome salt
his pegs know splintered feet,
a captain's sure as his
moorings thrown to lasso cleats

oh, the good captain!
alas, his sprite's blown away
for glass eyes that see wide pies
that lie crumbling in bays.

# Commissions to Write

buccaneers reigned
over seas
with majesty,
they traded eight
pieces for
opportunities

they were the
pirates
who drifted,
poets whose
pens danced
on seas
defending
gifted and
grifted
swindled thieves

they pillaged
and abridged
words of romance,
they were bilingual
and dueled with
their tongues
and swore to
French wenches
in Caribbean suns

they embraced
their peg legs
with billows
of sleeves, and
sea breezes
masked a smell
barons emit to
increase their
odds of finding
the world's keys

the things that
horizons
can't show like
naked orbs
eyes can't find
or naval
commissions
that steal to
justify eyes
that are blind

when an
illusion
of a
spherical
world was
trusted

buccaneers
offered
chivalry
in a world
where men
dueled
with pens in
the golden
age of
poetry

# Abject Fantasies

He was asked if he cared, no was kindly replied as
Though caring was even on the table
The seamen spared his feelings, hiding their disdain and smug
Contempt for him, and then came belligerence
And shrilled voices rose like the sea water so vain, so full of brine
And brimming to complain about ranks
So he found it prudent to lay low, to read letters sailors sent about
Figurines that danced erratically to a music box's
Wind, they clung to one or the other magnetically and were
Free, safe in castration's portal as a quill's quivers
Tend to be, when it drips and spots the fletching of cupid's arrows
Feathering the ocean's calms with tiny
Bows in hands that grew wrinkled like pruned limbs

And far beneath hands on deck a temptress haunts meek sailors
Daring them to look into medusa's eyes,
She preys on contemptuous souls, asking for their sumptuous bowls
Of gruel and she watches boils break
So fallacies rise, and then oarsmen asked and they were beaten
Like galley slaves, like zygotes get chances
To squiggle away with the stringy condom jellyfish that wiggle
Bravely past medusa's ovaries;

The first mate was emboldened, having learned the
Rigors of being tethered to a hollow mast.
He swaggered for submission, his legs bowed to higher
Ranks, on edges of blades he bled
And then babbled a meek confession to join their phalanx
"Does my opinion matter," he obsessed, "is it even solicitous to you?"
He asked if medusa cared what sailors made him do.

His mates checked on his tethered time, chortling at the idea that
Galley slaves could rain on parades of ranking men,
Who wager tides and the moon's tenacity, how it will shine medusas
Head to fit their dungarees, and they salivated
Watching her fellate lower ranks for 4 pieces of 8 that clung to
Hollow masts for bait in moon's brightest wanes

"Do my opinions matter? Or is it just your eyes as seen through you"
Fourth and third mates checked their watches, and the first one went free
"Vengeance is mine, sayeth me!" He called, as pirates began to plunder,
And wonder why their figurine village burned, and the vindication of
That satisfied him

# Knish Vendors

Amsterdam
felt useless,
it was empty
cold as light
inked red
across puddles

vacancy signs
knew desolation's
faces well,
bathing neon
with rhythms
their story's
lives could spell

and bums roamed
streets for dogs
lost for spays
and knish
vendors'
business went
to hookers
for lays

they lay on the track,
they ride the rails. . . .

Harlem shuffles
back A-trains
that near the
Apollo as
morning sun
pokes through to
feed the pimps
and homeless
actors it
grows.

# Finding Hucksters

trickling down
Nevada
Avenue
on parade,
she stood
in our
bathtub
to tap
tiles,

like an
offspring of
Harold Hill
she sang
"you've got
trouble
right hear
in river
city,"

she quoted
us an
exorbitant
cost,
I said
"whoa, ging-ga"
and her
sales pitch
ended
abruptly

she was
agitated,
pissed-off
and packed
up her woo-woo
sticks and
musical
sense for shtick,
her eyes
quivered
in anger's purse
like lips
of 76
trombones

# Avocations

a Jehovah's Witness
broke our step
stool, I guess
he needed
to get closer
to Him,

he had to
witness more
of his own
hand knocking
on our ceiling:

he apprenticed,
he claimed
he was a
jack–of– all– trades
so I spoke
cautiously

He pounded
and listened;
checking
for cracks
and fissures,
for sounds that
balanced
our stool

I feared I
might not see
him alone
again,
so I
began a
banter
about Vietnam
and their
contentious
objections

Jehovah
never came
through
the door,
across
thresholds,
through cracks
in our
ceiling

he tried
to fix things
he was trained
to see,
like measures
of moldy
ceilings
and his
objections
to war that
were of
interest to me.

# Good Saint Hugo

Cassocks wrinkle, diphthongs sound
Guttural until popes realize
Black smoke rising bold
From Vatican chimneys to
Holy skies Rome tries to hide

Silver hammers tap heads
That can nod, they writhe
And feel for traces of papal left,
Then call for silence as chalk
Scratches boards to nominate them

But they know Hugo Chávez is dead
So Buenos Aires steals their glory
From mist that steeps Argentina's
Sand to upstage history

And shores lick fierce at popes
Washing dead men's cassocks
Along the Tyrrhenian Sea,
Its tides cleanse whiter smoke
That thinned air Catholics know
Too well to change what time
Confesses to be.

# Life at the Party

I see where
agoraphobics
are coming from,
I know why
doors hide
them and
light waits
behind

peace of mind
finds a way
for foes
to handle
knobs of doors
leaving
party guests
wanting more

I understand
where pariahs
get gusto
and badges
worn for
fame that
fleets off coats
like rain

they were my
legions
then, fans who
shined my
knobs with twists
that proved
I wasn't
insane

so I tightened
thresholds
down, I
mended
reclusive ways
for now
to play host

like on game
shows no
one listens to,
the noise
in the back
room that
couldn't go
anywhere

I threw lame
parties
and hoped they
laughed, I
left them there
on my porch,
twisting,
begging for more

# Catch 22 + 1 = skidoo

Blessed are the dignitaries, the individuals who toiled and perfected their trade
Blessed are criminals who surrendered their guns so an ounce
Of dignity was saved

Toughness guided thieves in Wal-Mart past greeters who give a retired nod
Toward experiences that wait in line while merchants twitter calloused hands
Behind counters servicing lips held to purse
And ask "are you experienced?"

The rhetoric of Hendrix is lost on them in their youth and
The employers expect an answer
So cross-trained flunkies can excel, magically they're pulled from pools
In panic and desperation

Hire applicants who float right by the twitters, they gain experience
From hairs they find in drains, blessed are the criminals
Who catch and neglect the system's flaws

Rouges that wave guns at store clerks, angry men who rant at night stockers
And pucker lips to deflect the pink slips management
Cannot afford

# Blindfold and Cigarette

it was always
there— winking
at me—
loathsomely
and I pled
what have I done,
or perhaps
I'll ask what
have you
become?

are you
envious
enough to
covet one,
am I asking
too much
much too
that I have
some?

one thing
to excel at,
hackneyed
words to edit
and spell
wrong the best
I can. . .

But, but
look at you
and all
you've done,
all I might
envy

I don't
because
life's too short
not to give
credit
to whom
it's due
and for what
is won,
like the
citations
and small timer's
awards
when we were
too young;

if I envied
you I might
ponder. . .
I'd muse
whether
it'd be
prudent to
talk beyond
repeated words,
whether
fear would be
bold enough
to walk
beyond
retreated
steps, but
that wouldn't be me
I wouldn't be me

I'd wonder
whether
I'd be cool
enough to
revolve
through doors
with jobs,
or if I could
just reach
out and
gouge the
eyes to see,
but that
wouldn't be me
I wouldn't be me

although
I might be
inclined to
envy you,
if I could have
notoriety
or paths life's
led you from. . .

eh. . . I guess
all that
stuff wasn't
meant to be,

like a golf
ball life
is played
where it lies,
too short
and coarse
to be petty
with picks
chosen at
random
tees

I envy you. . .

your motivation
and discipline
that shows and
then tells things
like they were

I envy you. . .

your transportation—
your modus
operandi—
but I doubt
I'd go anywhere
if I coveted
you, but
I'm a winner
so I spin
my wheels
indefatigably
and muddle
through.

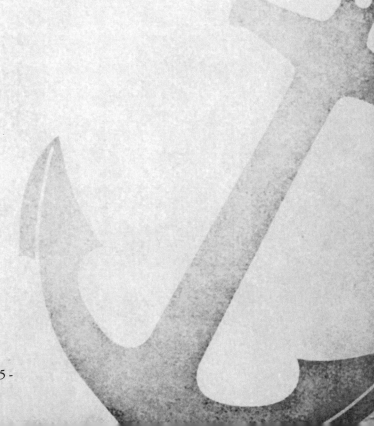

# About the Author

Author Michael P Amram acquired a Bachelor of Arts degree from the University of Minnesota- Duluth in 1989. Since graduating he has been writing fiction, poetry and non-fiction. In 1998 Amram saw his first publication with a short- story "The Den of Antiquities." In 2003 he sold an excerpt from a short story to accompany an article featured in the Canadian magazine Abilities. A portion of the manuscript for his first novel, *The Orthodoxy of Arrogance* (Trafford 2013), was submitted for the 2011-12 mentor program run by the Loft Literary Center in Minneapolis, Minnesota. His work was selected from seventy-eight other fiction writers to be a finalist. Between October 2013 and June 2014 he published two novels and two poetry collections. He is currently working on a memoir titled *Growing up DFL: A Memoir of Minnesota Politics during the Vietnam War.* He and his wife live in St. Louis Park, Minnesota. Much of his published and unpublished work can be found at www.michaelpaulamram.weebly.com.

Printed in the United States
By Bookmasters